JOHN R. ANDERSON | *Explored*

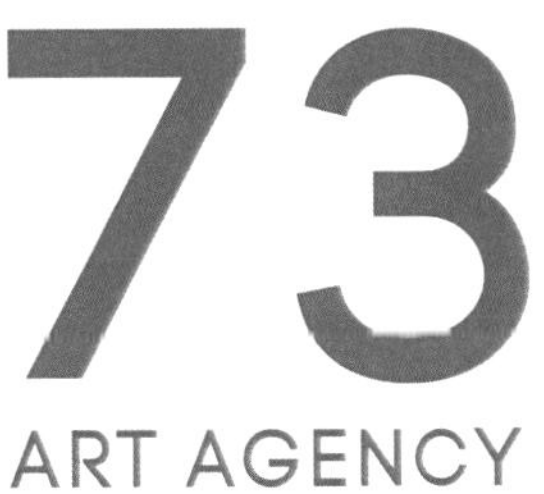

JOHN R. ANDERSON | *Explored*

73 Art Agency
Denver, Colorado
info@73artagency.com
www.73artagency.com

Front Cover: *276*, Acrylic on canvas (framed), 1999–2009, 45 x 39 in (115 x 99 cm)

ISBN 978-1-950484-06-5

Published by Spring Cedars
Denver, Colorado
www.springcedars.com

We are pleased to present this new selection of work by artist John R. Anderson. It features 51 abstract acrylic paintings from across the artist's career, including two early paintings from the 1960s, eight from the 1990s, and sixteen completed recently in 2018. This catalogue explores Anderson's artistic process and technique, offering fresh insights into the artist's unique art and creative development.

John R. Anderson's work is an exceptional source for research and public delight. With this catalogue we hope to generate art inquiry and discovery while encouraging the celebration of original art.

We are grateful to all who have contributed both directly and indirectly to this exhibition and catalogue. Special thanks to Christine Anderson without whom not much would come to fruition.

73 Art Agency

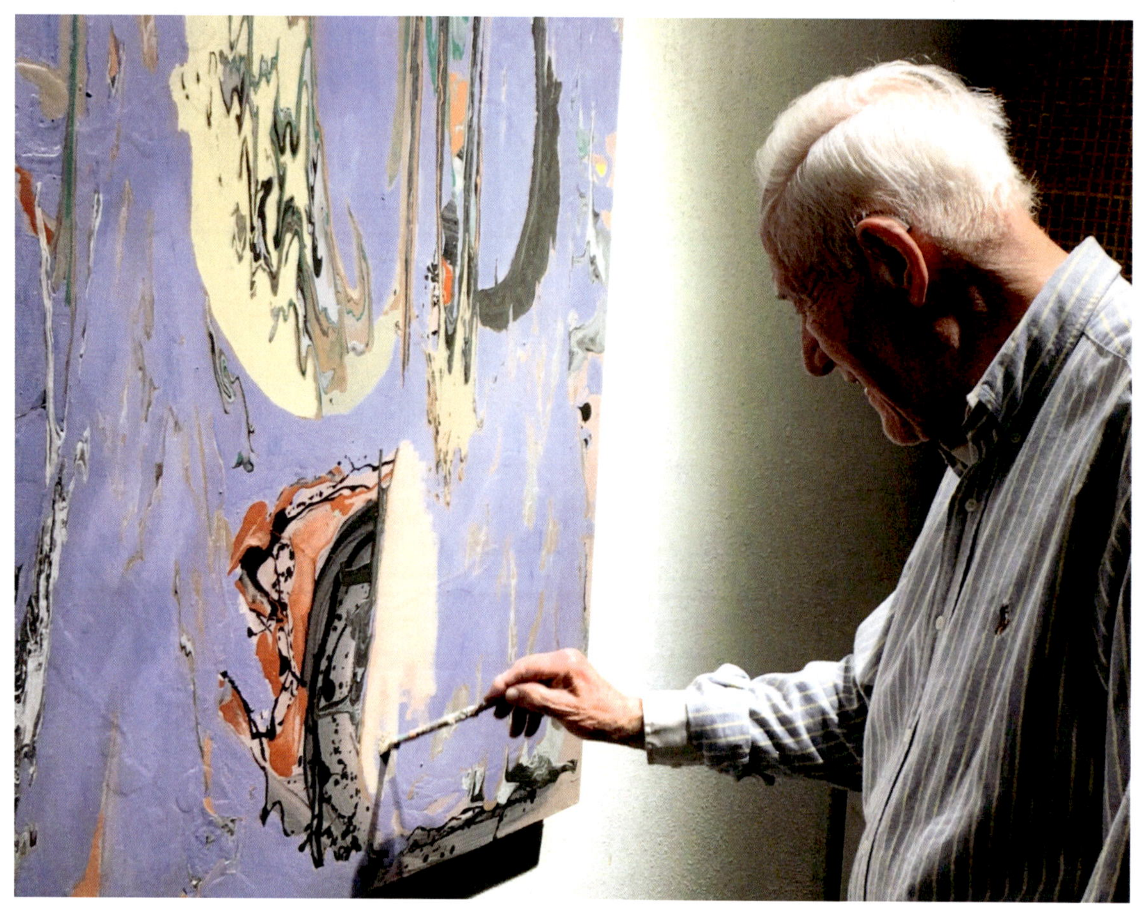

Anderson at work, 2018

John R. Anderson was born in Yankton, South Dakota, in 1931. As a student of the Minneapolis School of Fine Arts, he participated in Oskar Kokoschka's symposia in 1952, then earned his BFA at the University of Denver School of Art in 1958, when Vance Kirkland was its director. In the late 1960s, Anderson painted extensively in Mexico, inspired by pre-Columbian art. He held his first major show at the Guadalajara Jalisco State Gallery, however, the revolutionary abstract art was met with overtly hostile criticism. Anderson moved to London to pursue his artistic aspirations. In 1971, he returned to Yankton to paint in isolation as he developed a deep and authentic form of personal expression. Although Anderson held a solo show at the Yankton Area Arts Association at G.A.R. Hall in 2009, his mystifying story and paintings remained hidden from the rest of the world.

In November 2017, a 73 Art Agency team traveled to meet Anderson and tour his studio. In April 2018, 51 of his lyrical abstract paintings were selected and showcased for the exhibition *Uncovered* in Colorado. In 2019, works presented in this catalogue were shown at the 73 Art Agency Skybox. In March 2020, a selection of paintings was displayed at The South Dakota Art Museum and two acquired for the museum's permanent art collection.

Anderson currently lives in Yankton, South Dakota, and continues to paint.

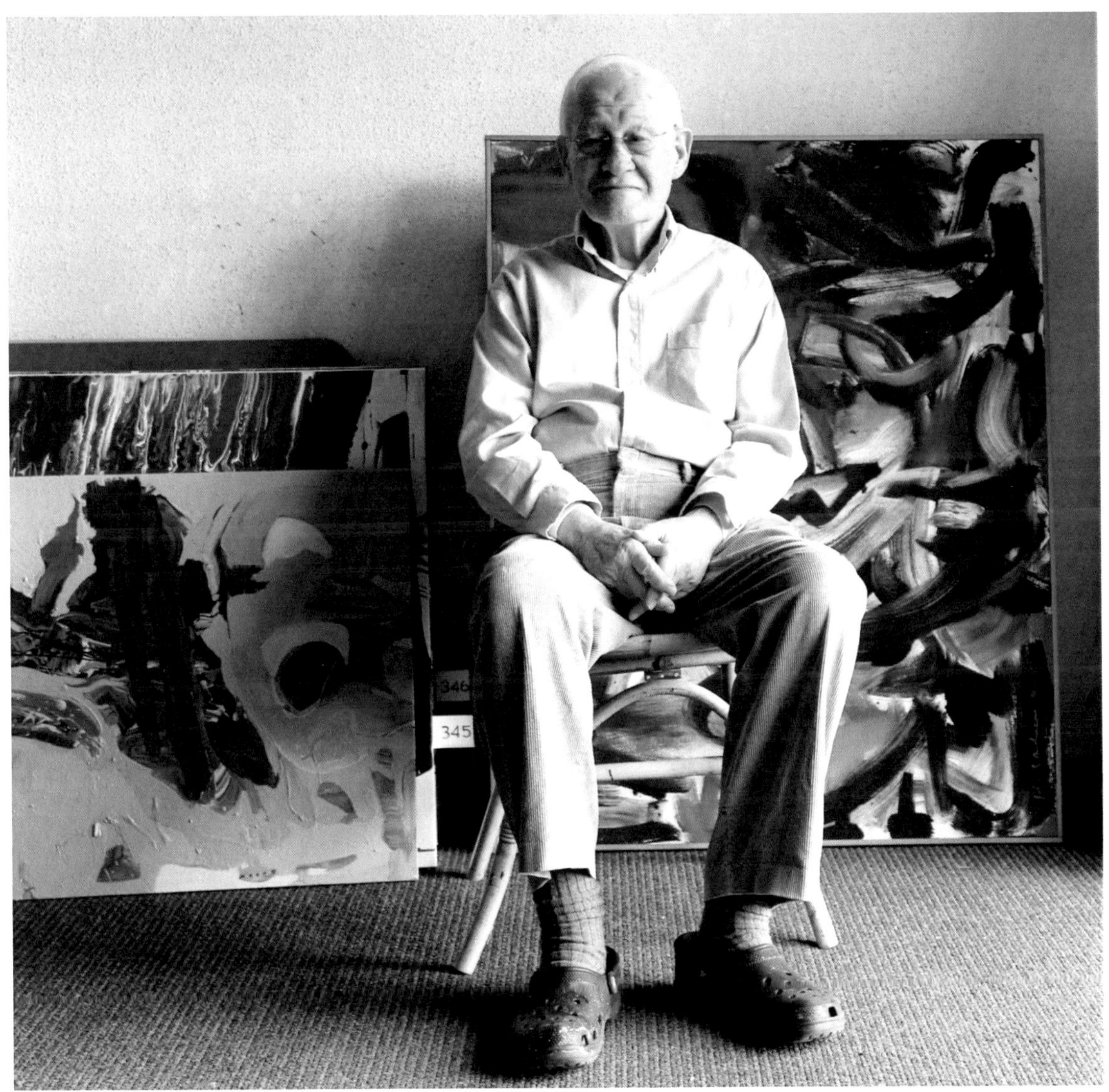

Yankton, 2018

"In those days it was hit or miss, people did not understand abstract work. But I've always wanted to paint and you just have to go with your experience and your own likes and dislikes."
~ John R. Anderson

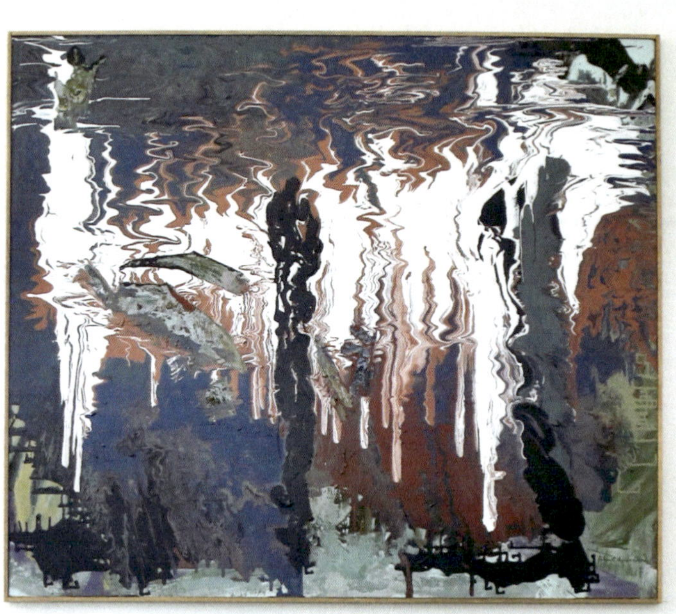

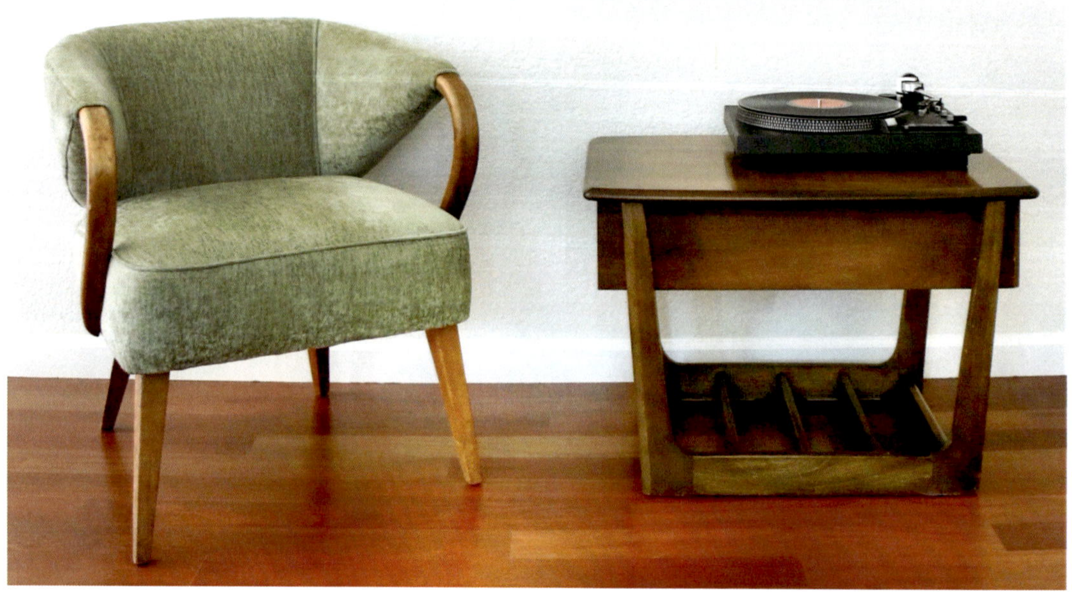

277 in Private Collection, 2020

JOHN R. ANDERSON: TECHNIQUE AND PROCESS

The remarkable discovery of John R. Anderson's œuvre in 2017 by 73 Art Agency has generated profound fascination within the art community and general public. Anderson's pure lyrical abstract paintings are a work in progress since the 1960's. Although **Lyrical Abstraction** is a critical artistic movement that has been largely overlooked within the post-Abstract Expressionist era, the uncovering of Anderson's work has provided a significant opportunity to re-initiate the dialogue. In 2018, 73 Art Agency presented fifty-one lyrical abstract acrylic paintings in the exhibition **Uncovered**, revealing the hidden artwork for the first time and placing it within the art historical context. **Explored**, featuring an additional fifty-one paintings, offers a deeper investigation of Anderson's artistic technique and process.

Anderson painted with oils in his earlier works, as seen with *2* and *The Gift*. In the late 1960s, he transitioned to **acrylics**, a synthetic medium made of pigments suspended in acrylic polymer emulsion. Acrylics, which create a matte waterproof film and show little color change when dried, provide unique characteristics including versatility, immediacy, and durability. Having the properties of both oils and watercolors, acrylic paint can be thinned with water and used to create a transparent glaze, or built into layers to create a dense opaque impasto. Anderson capitalizes on the ability to modify the consistency of acrylics, applying thin hues as well as thick colors, building both soft and hard textured elements. All of his paintings include the strong colors, the sharp strokes, and the quality lines that acrylic paint offers. "It had to be acrylic," the artist affirms.

Anderson's lyrical abstract technique involves **first layer**, **flow**, **simplification**, and **shaping**; these elements, however, are not all always present. He places the canvas on the floor to achieve the flow effect and works on an easel or against a wall for first layer, simplification, and shaping. When working on the floor, Anderson pours the paint directly onto the canvas, a technique known as "**accidental painting**." The artist spills layers of different colors, allowing the paint to coalesce into unexpected patterns, as seen in *289*. Anderson also drips pigments, visibly in *226*, or smears layers of paint across the surface of the canvas with a cloth, as in *248*. Anderson seriously begins to explore flow in the 1990s, after deciding to forgo acrylic tubes for tubs, as demonstrated in *276*. "Everything changed when I started buying gallons of paint," Anderson explains, "I lay the canvas on the floor and poured, and one thing led to another. I'd lift one end and let it flow, lift another end and let it flow." He rotates the canvas and changes the direction of a painting over time, playing with movement.

When working on the easel or against a wall, Anderson dilutes the acrylic paint with water and uses a brush to create washes such as in *39*. He also sets thick layers of paint directly from the tube to build impastos, very markedly in *59.1*. "You see," says Anderson as he points to *The Enemy is Us*, "brush has its place. It's amazing some of the effects." He uses brushwork for an initial layer, as well as to both simplify and shape his work. Simplification, according to Anderson, consists of "toning down" the painting with white or muted earth tones, *104* offering a great example. "I often go in with the white to illuminate [the image] and accentuate the good movement... with a small brush and a lot of patience," Anderson describes, "I go in on the wall and simplify. I leave the strong elements and make them stand out." Conversely, for shaping, Anderson applies accents of bold pigments and strokes onto the surface of the canvas, as in *160*. "I add bright colors and change the shapes to build contrast and to give [the painting] a subtle zing," he says. Through the juxtaposition of simplification and shaping, Anderson explores a Lyrical Abstract paradox. "The colors are muted and subtle, then, zing! There's brightness and intensity," the artist reveals, "it's tamed, but it's wild."

With the unique characteristics of acrylic paint and the use of various techniques, the actual process becomes more present and relevant. As a Lyrical Abstractionist, Anderson works with **color**, **form**, and **texture** to build a visual rhythm through personal movement, expression, and freedom. The contrasting values and lines of Anderson's painting are powerfully and dynamically produced, much like the varying tones and keys of a piano concerto. The artist does not start a painting in any particular way nor does he follow a specific procedure. "It all comes from working with it and how I feel. It has to come from within," the artist explains, "and sometimes I really go wild, and I don't know why I do particular things. I just feel that it has to be done." Anderson's creative process is a conflicting combination of **structured rational applications** and **emotional unexplainable actions**. "My job is to build and make sensible decisions over time, and coming to a point of control is a long learning process with lots of trial and error. I work and rework. It's a real progression," he says. The numerous dates recorded on the back of his canvases attest to this approach, as seen on the back of *26*. Anderson takes several years to reach a desired expression. "But there also comes a point of over-painting, and knowing when to stop is essential. [...] It's especially important not to over-think."

Anderson is most pleased with his work when he is able to explore new processes, the paintings "are strong because I've gone into new territory. I took a new approach that was successful. [...] When I enter new ground...the color, the space, the movement...you know, Bam Bam! Slam Bam! And it works! […] there's an aura. It just lives." Anderson describes that the mood changes from painting to painting depending on pigments, texture, design, as well as the viewer. Indeed, no two paintings look or feel alike, and no two viewers will have the same reaction or interpretation. Anderson, who numbers his paintings, is adamant about allowing his audience to make up their own mind about the art. "I don't like to put words in your mouth," he says. "All of these paintings are unique, and my personal feelings for one painting against another varies, and that is no sign that one is better than the other. You just have to go with your experience and your own likes and dislikes. It's all up to you!"

Audrey Zurcher
University of Denver, BA '17

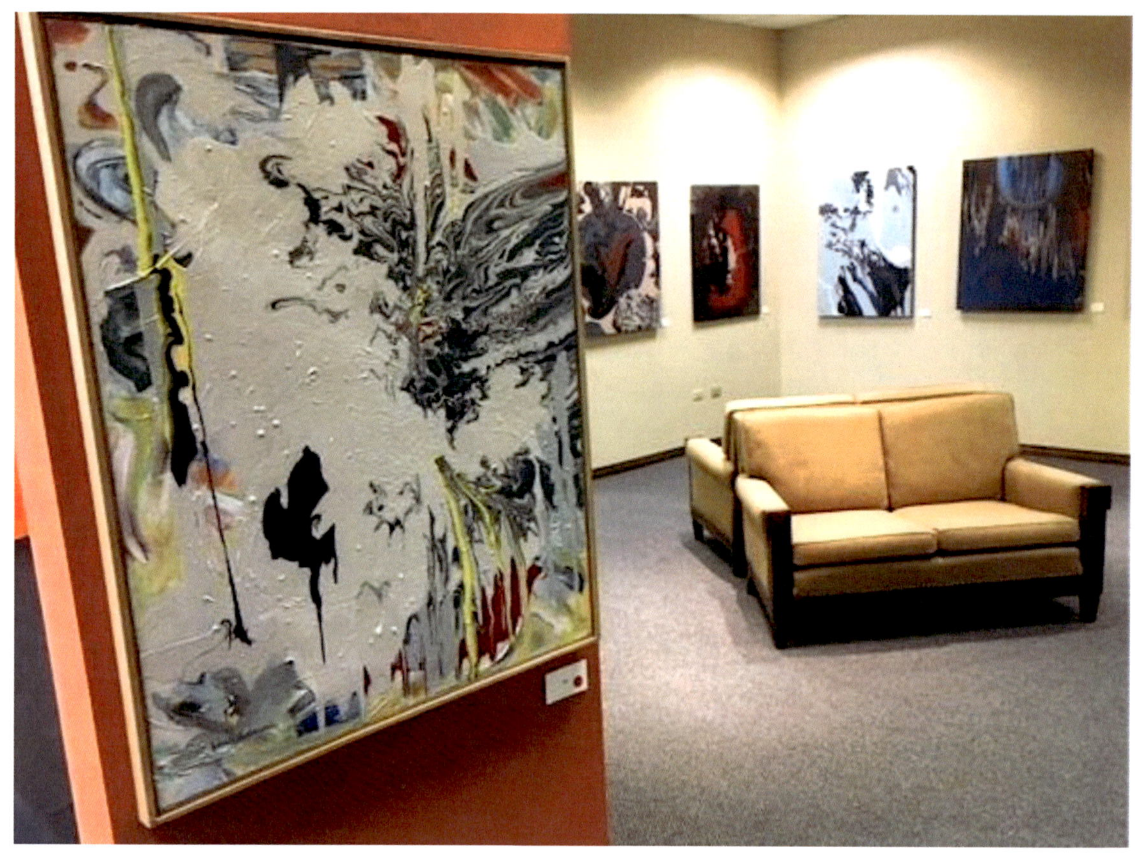

John R. Anderson *Uncovered* exhibition, 2018

“The combinations of poured, scraped and brushed layers of paint are a part of a process of call and response, an intuitive and critical engagement with decision-making. Anderson works intuitively in response to process and looks for the right balance between conscious control and instinctual excitement.”
~ South Dakota Art Museum

“These paintings are beautiful. They remind me of the best mid-century abstract works now hanging in major museums world-wide: the intuitive, sensual, loose and harmonious compilation of design, brushwork, and color that defines this genre. In each piece, I see something new. I feel something raw. I sense a playful experimentation. Each painting exhibits a deep knowledge of color theory and harmony. This engrossing body of work from this prolific artist is sophisticated, intriguing, and original. I am impressed. I am hooked.”
~ Kathryn Marsh Riedinger, Award-winning Painter and Plein Air Art Instructor

WORKS

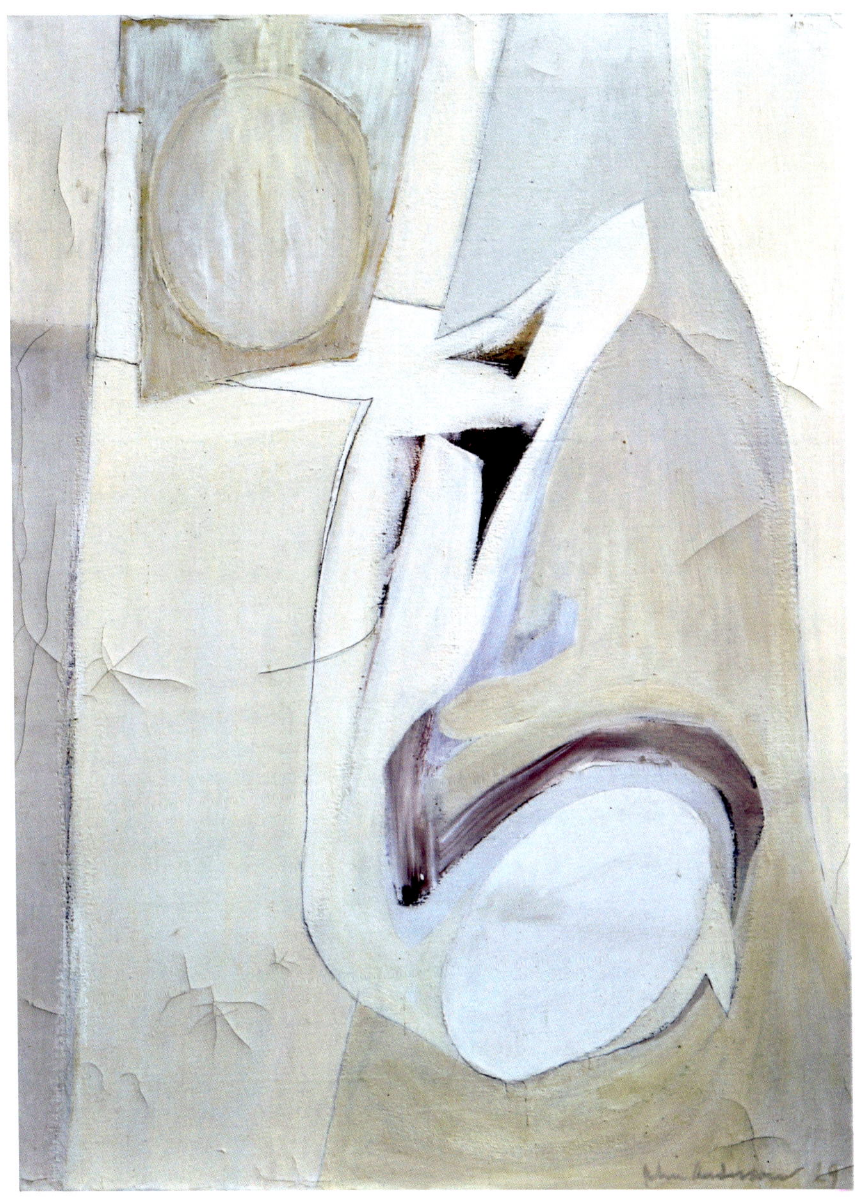

2
Oil and pencil on canvas (framed)
1969
38 x 28 in (97 x 71 cm)

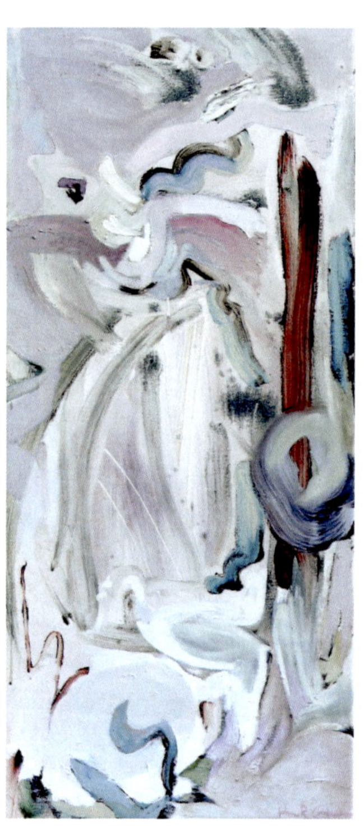

3
Acrylic on canvas (framed)
1991-2018
42 x 22.3 in (122 x 57 cm)

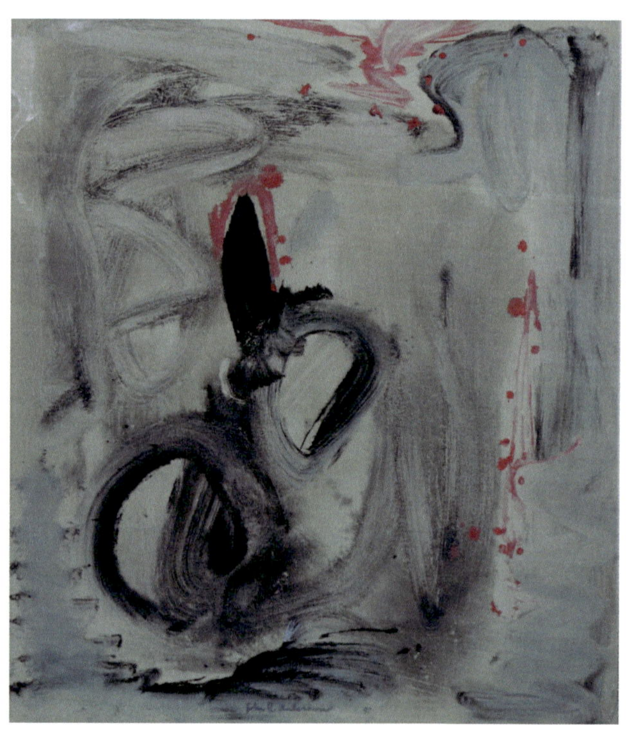

6
Acrylic on canvas (framed)
1992
38 x 34 in (97 x 87 cm)

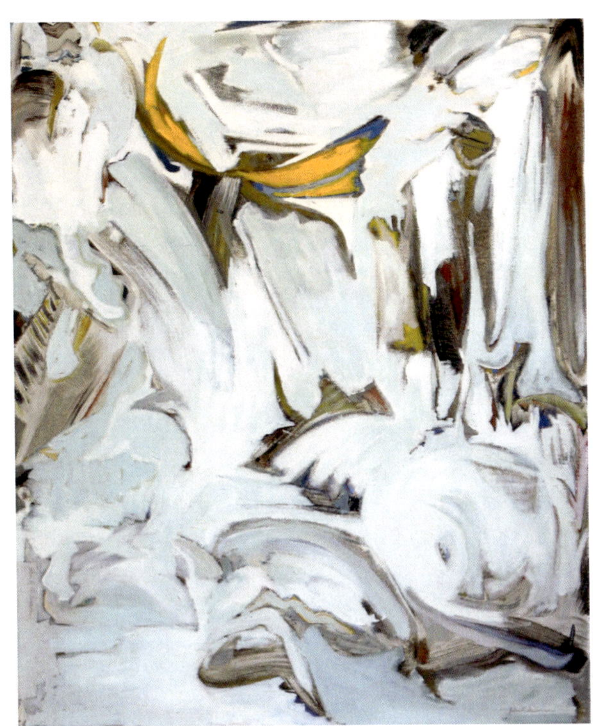

26
Acrylic on canvas (framed)
1998–2001
53 x 45 in (135 x 115 cm)

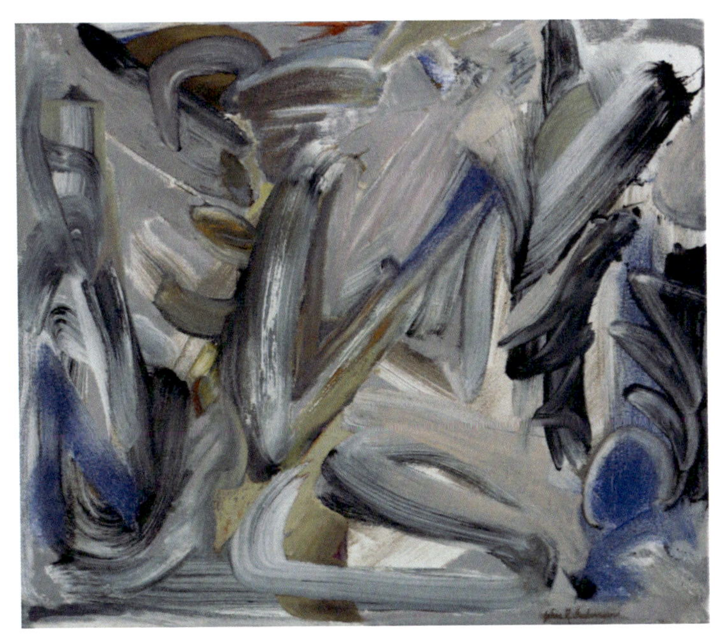

33
Acrylic on canvas (framed)
1991–1994
29 x 34.5 in (74 x 88 cm)

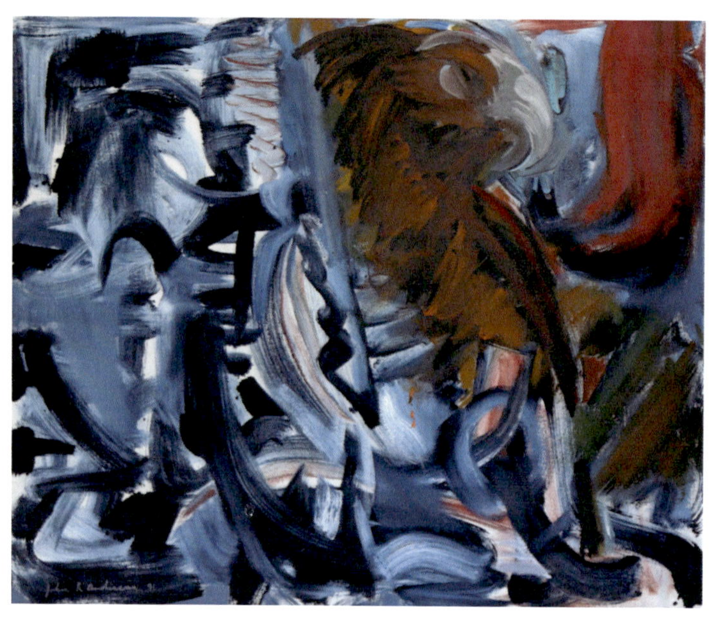

38
Acrylic on canvas (framed)
1991
36 x 44 in (92 x 112 cm)

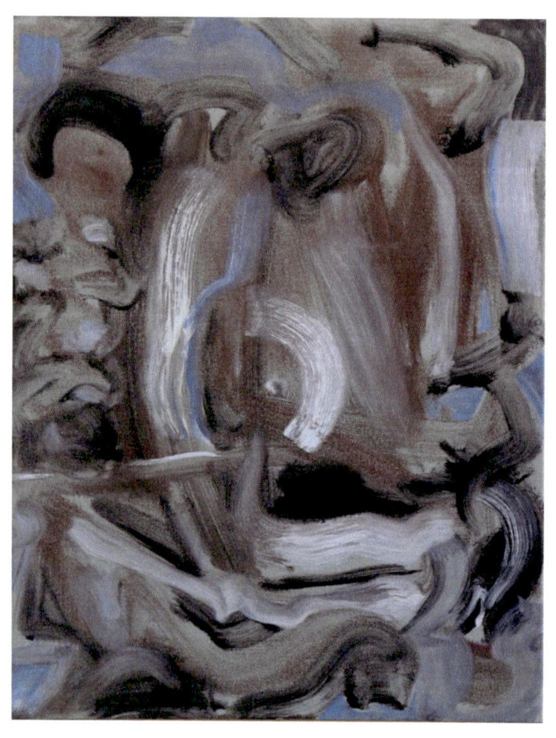

39
Acrylic on canvas (framed)
1991
40.5 x 32 in (103 x 82 cm)

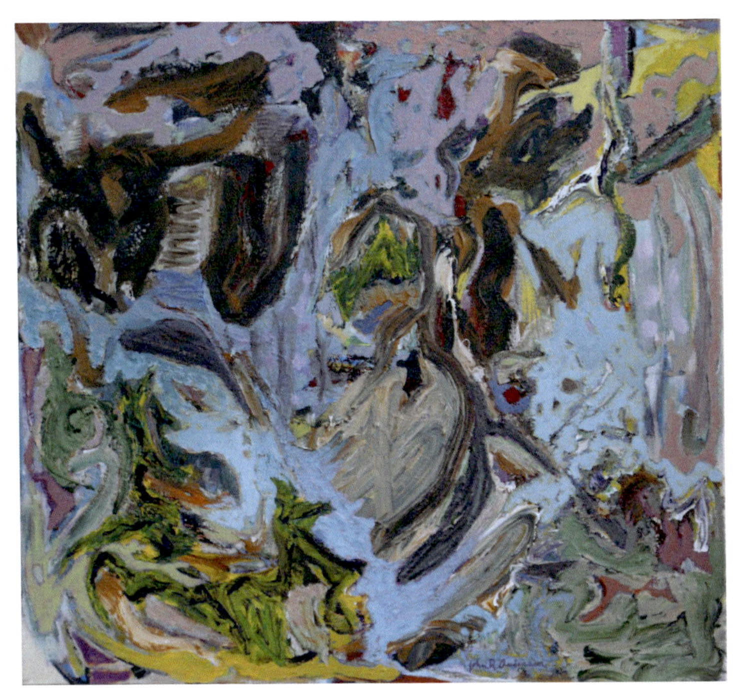

59.1
Acrylic on canvas (framed)
1996–2013
35 x 32 in (89 x 82 cm)

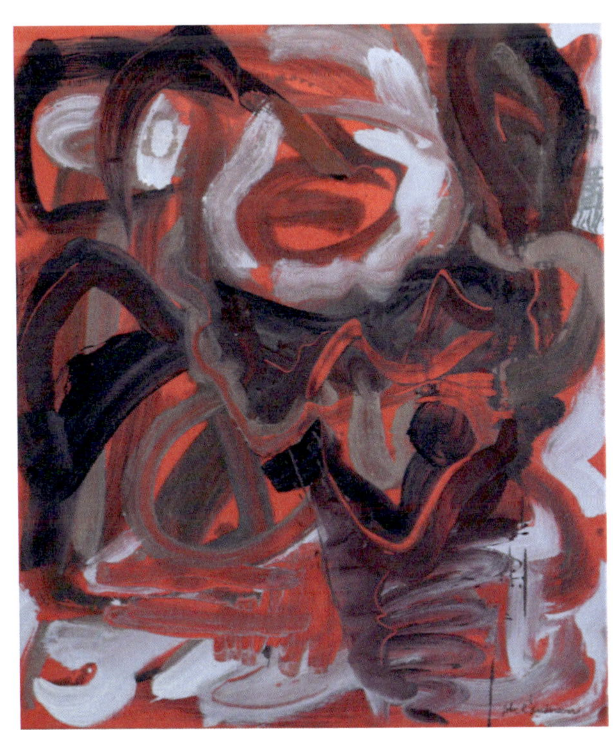

76
Acrylic on canvas (framed)
1991
37.8 x 32.8 in (96 x 83 cm)

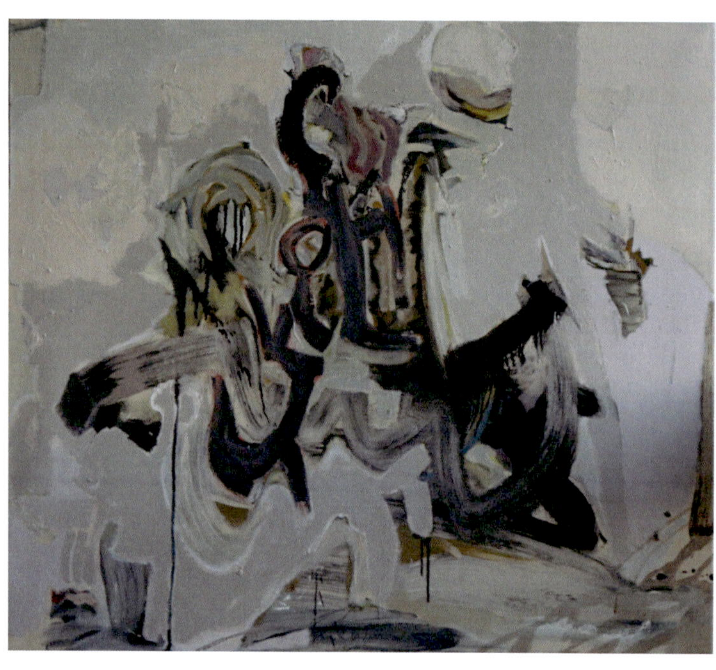

104
Acrylic on canvas (framed)
1996–2018
40 x 45.5 in (100 x 116 cm)

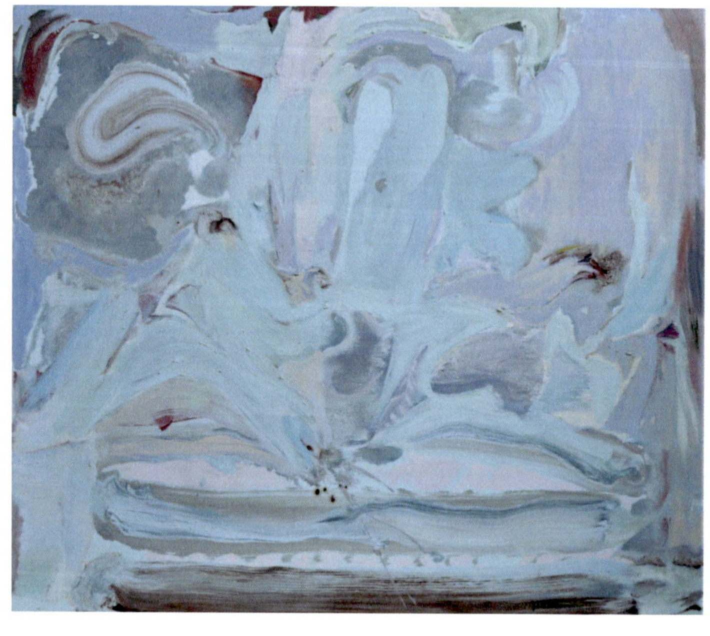

119
Acrylic on canvas
1997
44 x 52 in (112 x 132 cm)

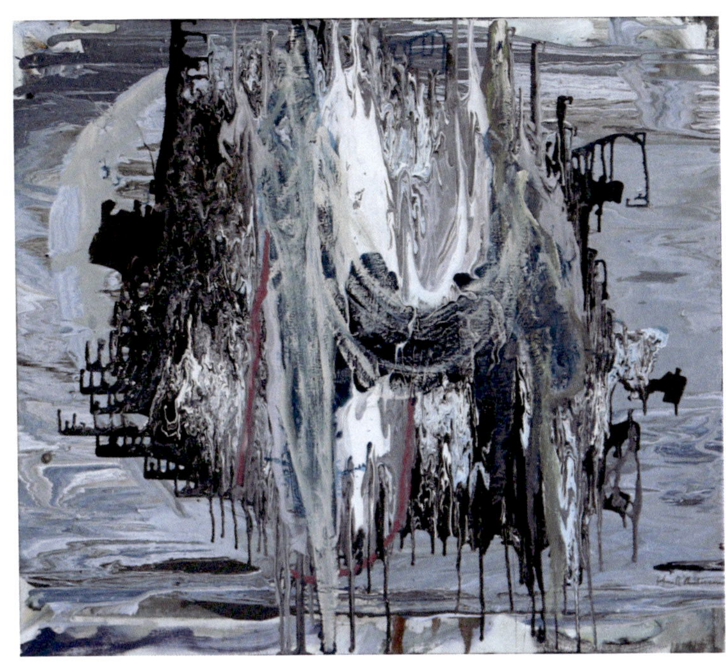

151
Acrylic on canvas (framed)
1999–2012
34 x 39 in (87 x 99 cm)

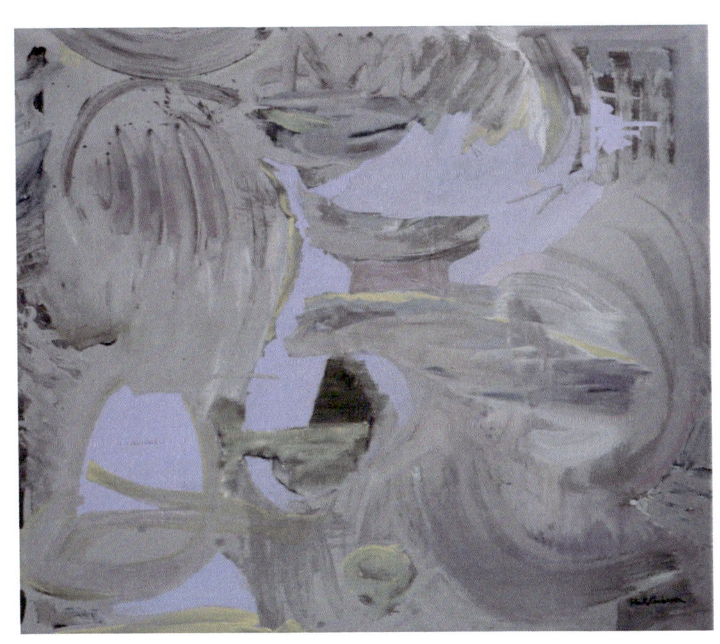

155
Acrylic on canvas (framed)
1998–2018
44 x 52 in (112 x 132 cm)

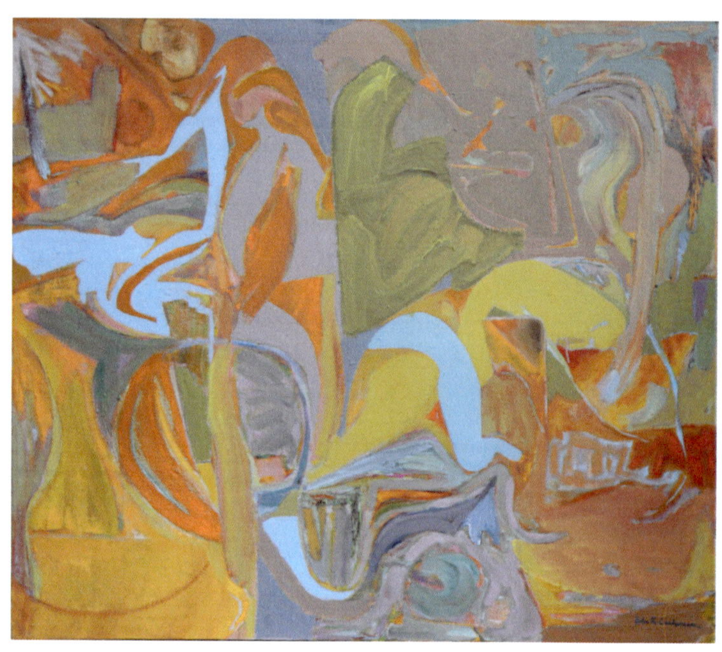

160
Acrylic on canvas
2005–2014
48 x 56 in (122 x 142 cm)

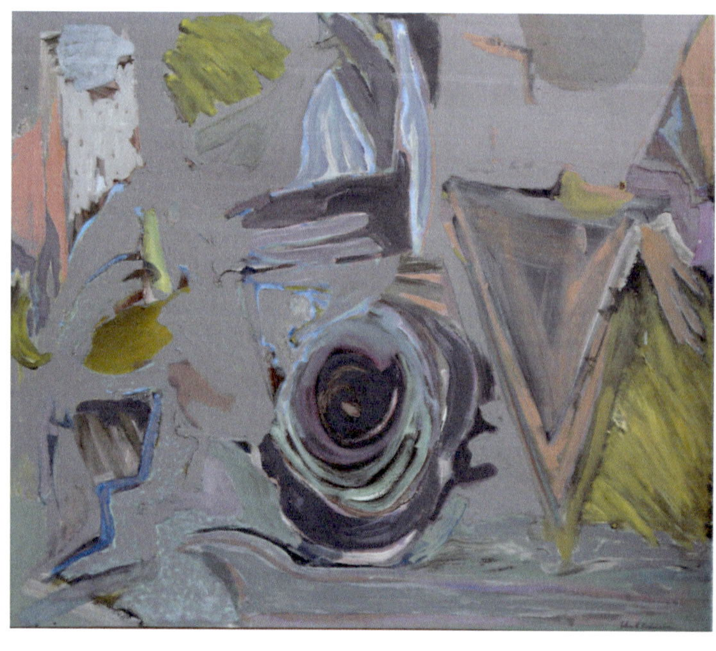

161
Acrylic on canvas (framed)
1998–2018
44 x 52 in (112 x 132 cm)

172
Acrylic on canvas (framed)
2007–2017
52 x 39 in (132 x 99 cm)

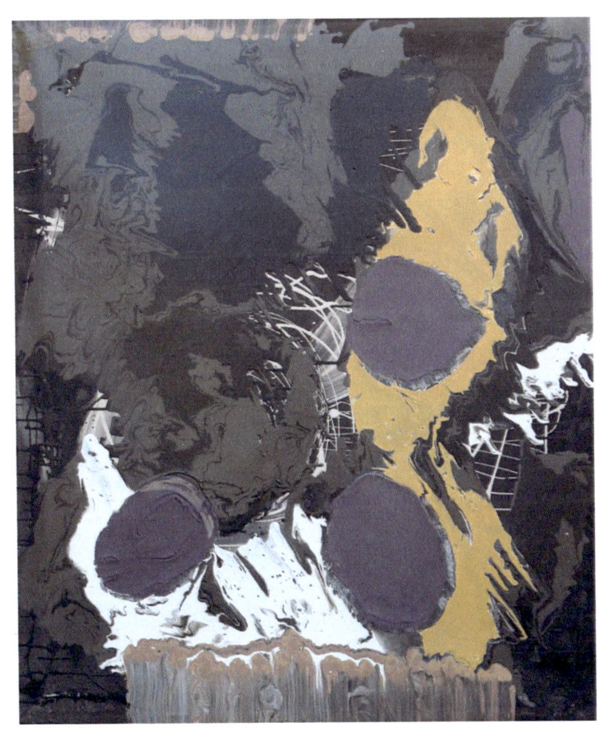

173
Acrylic on canvas
2007–2011
52 x 44 in (132 x 112 cm)

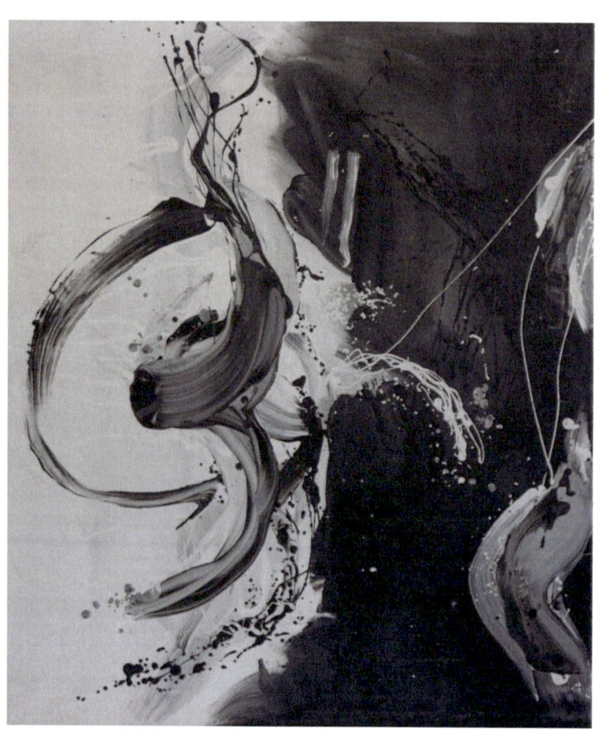

176
Acrylic on canvas
2007
46 x 39.5 in (117 x 101 cm)

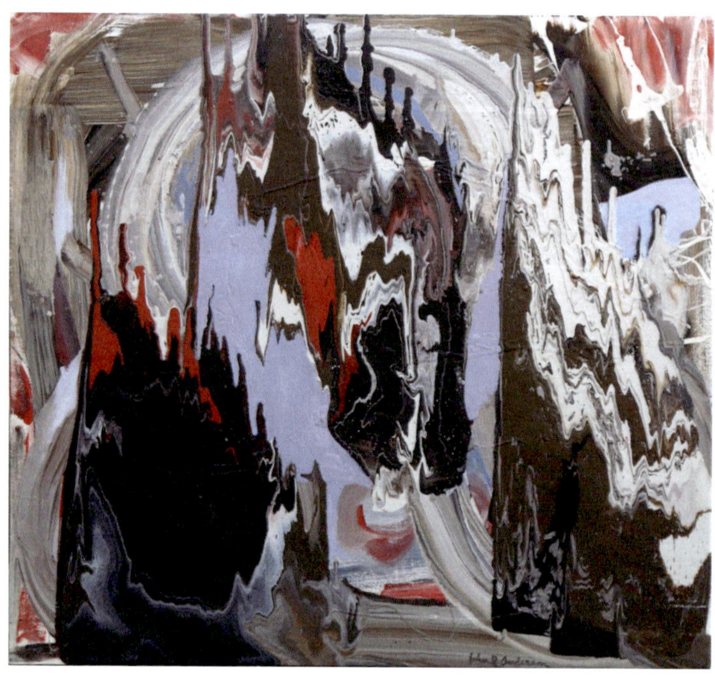

187
Acrylic on canvas
2008–2009
34 x 38 in (87 x 97 cm)

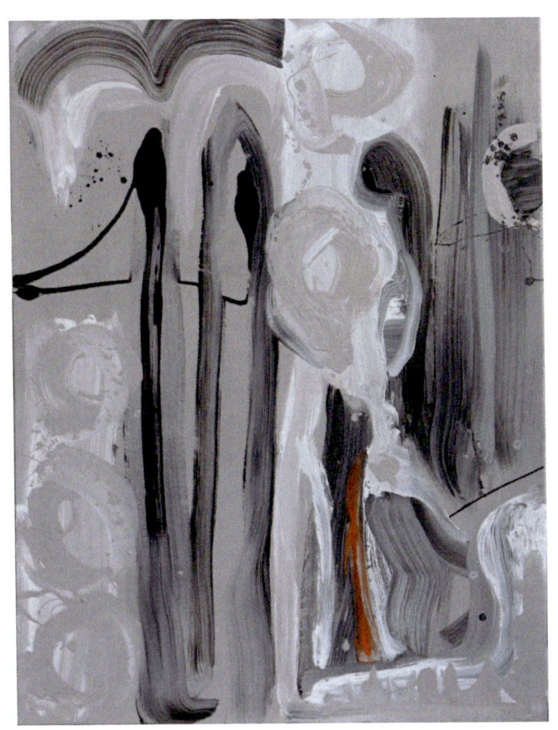

192
Acrylic on canvas
2008
50 x 39 in (127 x 99 cm)

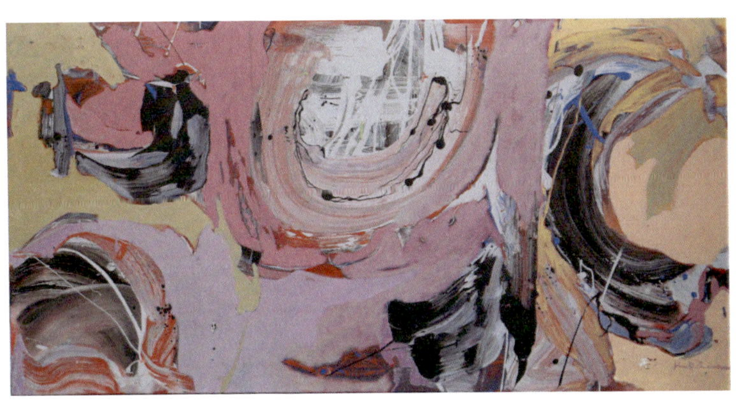

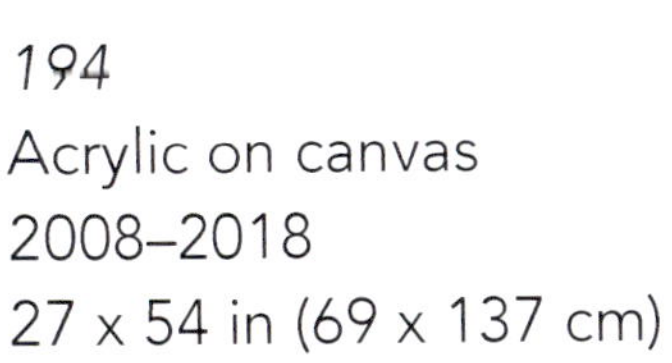

194
Acrylic on canvas
2008–2018
27 x 54 in (69 x 137 cm)

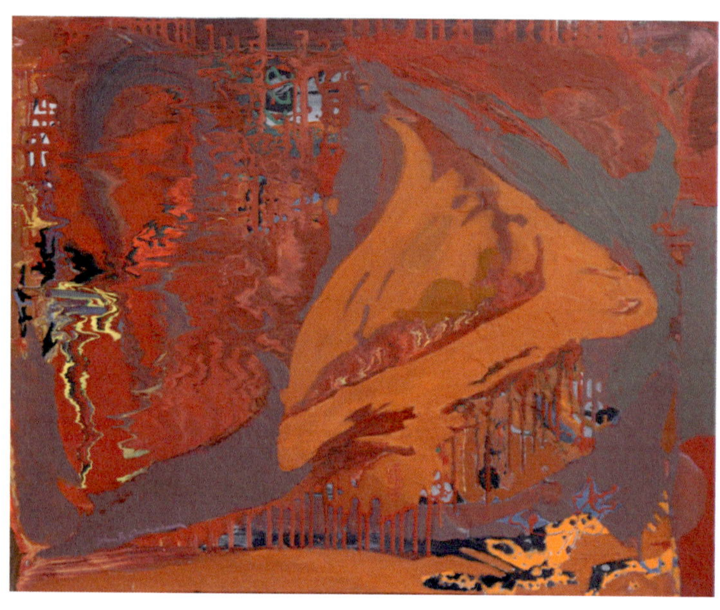

197
Acrylic on canvas
2008–2016
32 x 41 in (82 x 104 cm)

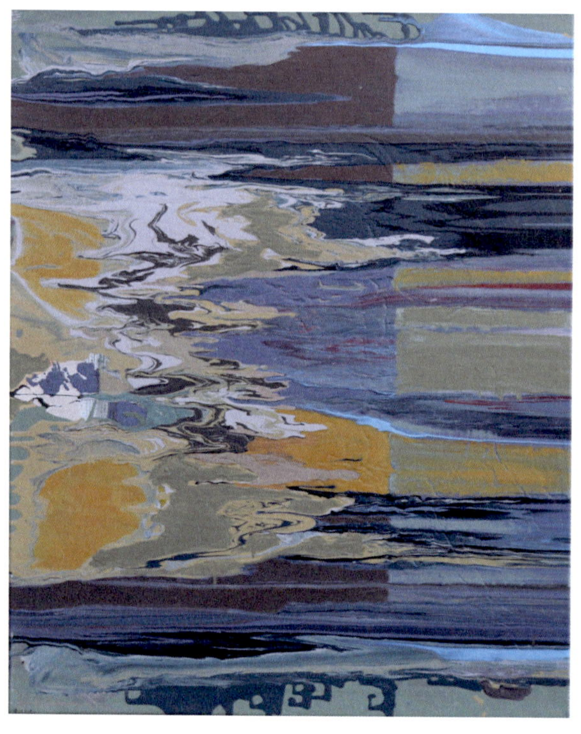

207
Acrylic on canvas
2008–2015
36 x 30 in (92 x 76 cm)

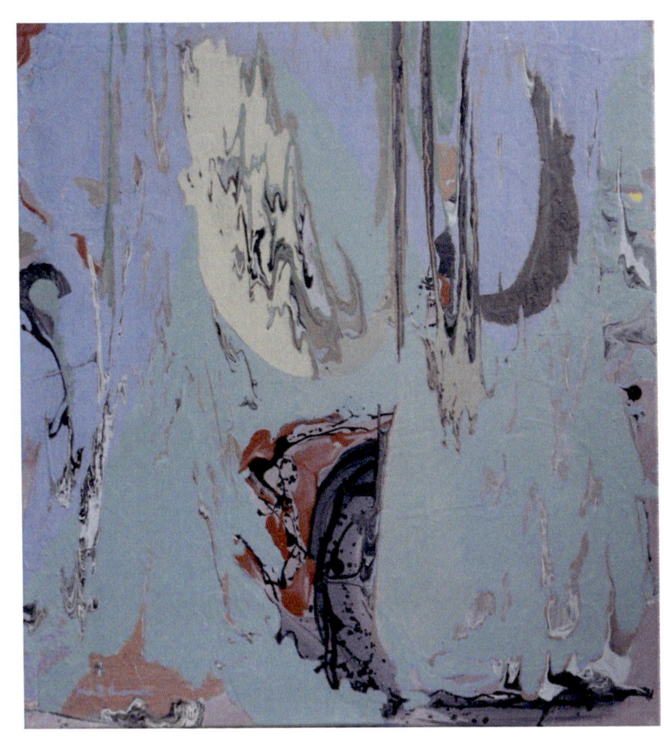

219
Acrylic on canvas
2008–2018
36.5 x 34 in (93 x 87 cm)

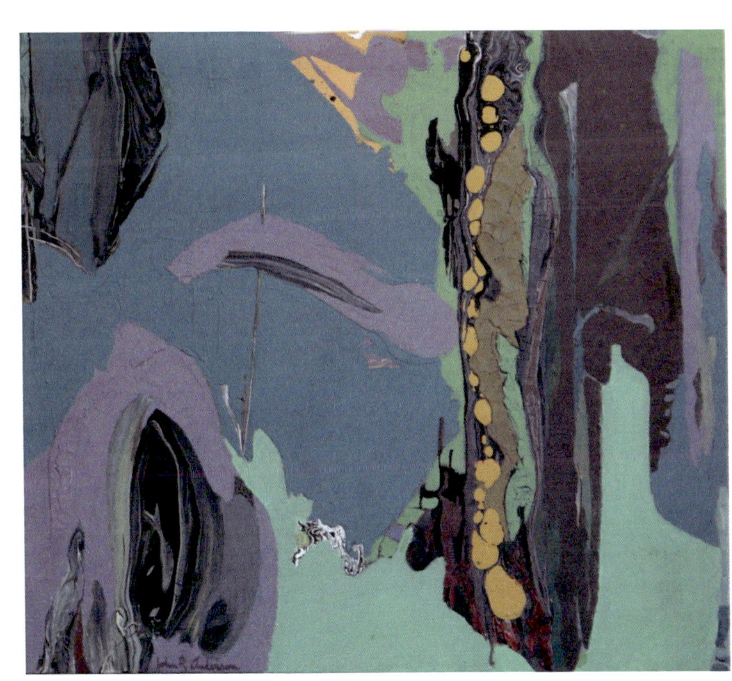

223
Acrylic on canvas
2008–2018
36 x 41 in (92 x 104 cm)

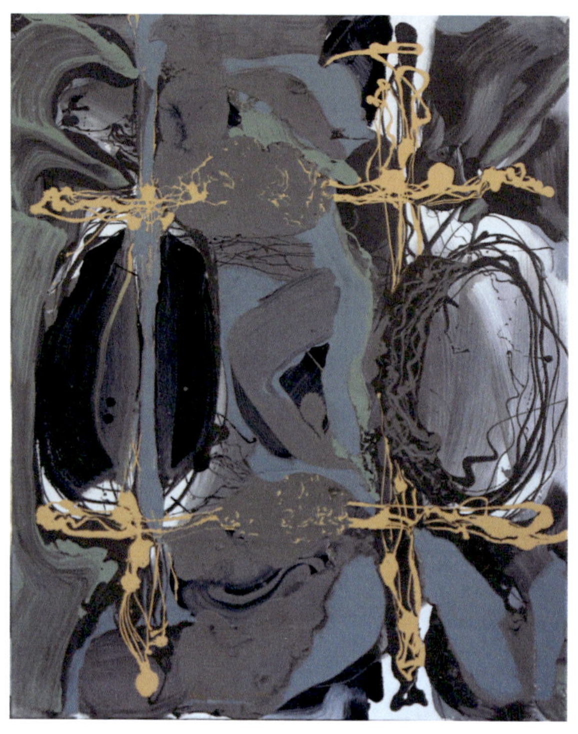

226
Acrylic on canvas
2008–2011
46 x 38 in (117 x 97 cm)

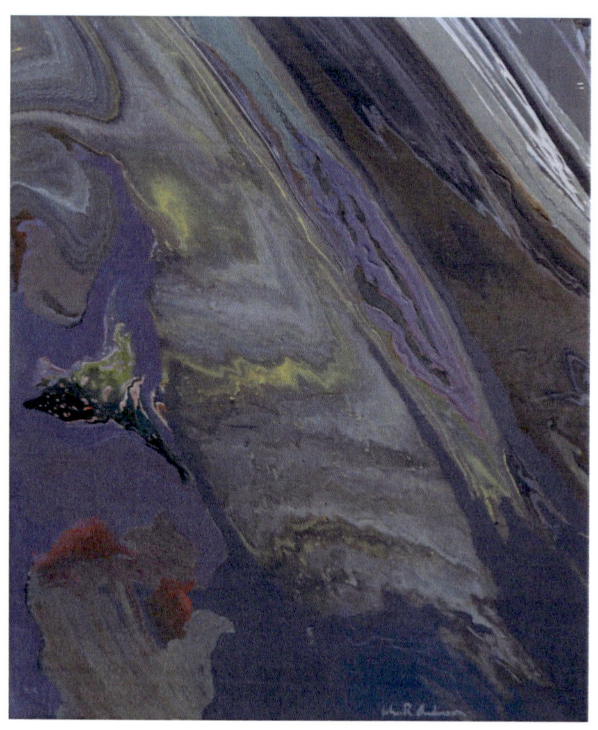

228
Acrylic on canvas
2008–2010
40 x 34 in (102 x 87 cm)

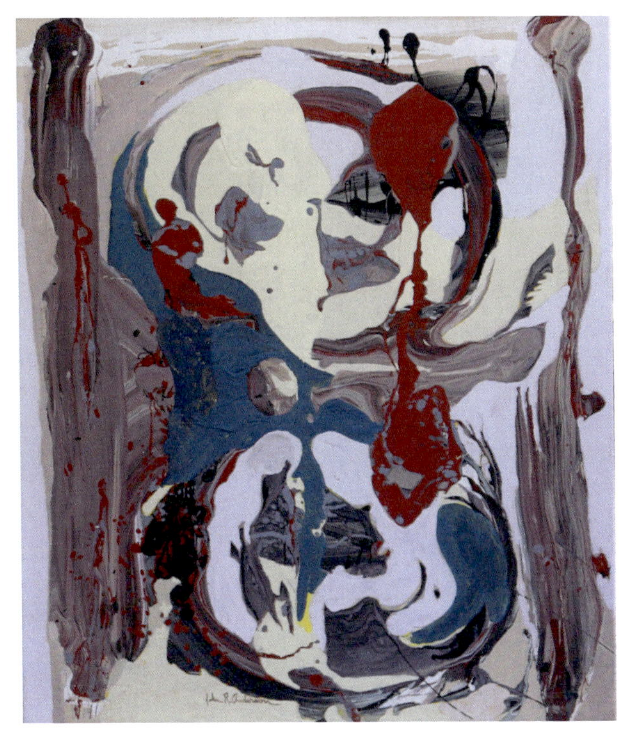

239
Acrylic on canvas
2009–2017
46 x 40 in (117 x 102 cm)

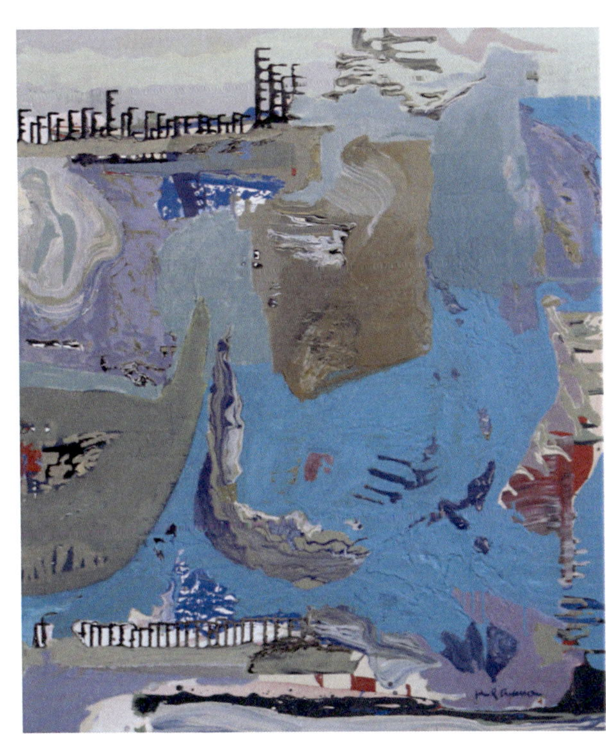

241
Acrylic on canvas
2009–2018
46 x 40 in (117 x 102 cm)

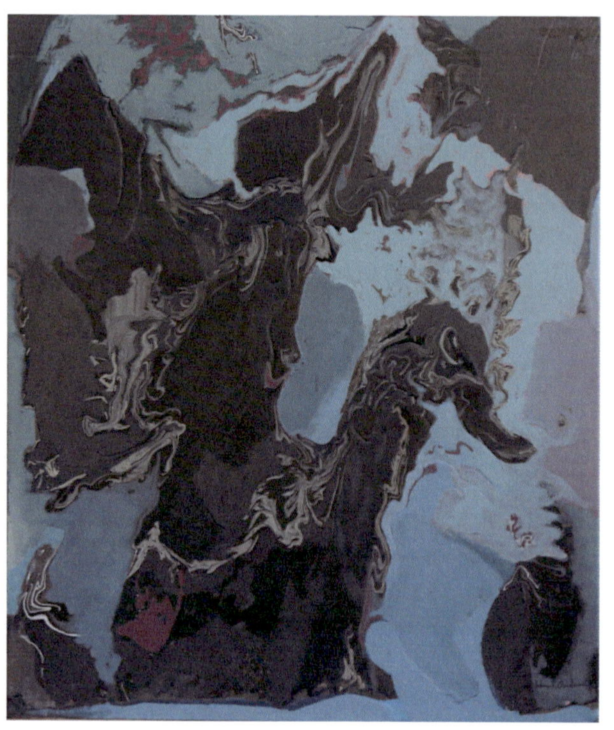

245
Acrylic on canvas (framed)
1992–2012
41 x 36 in (104 x 92 cm)

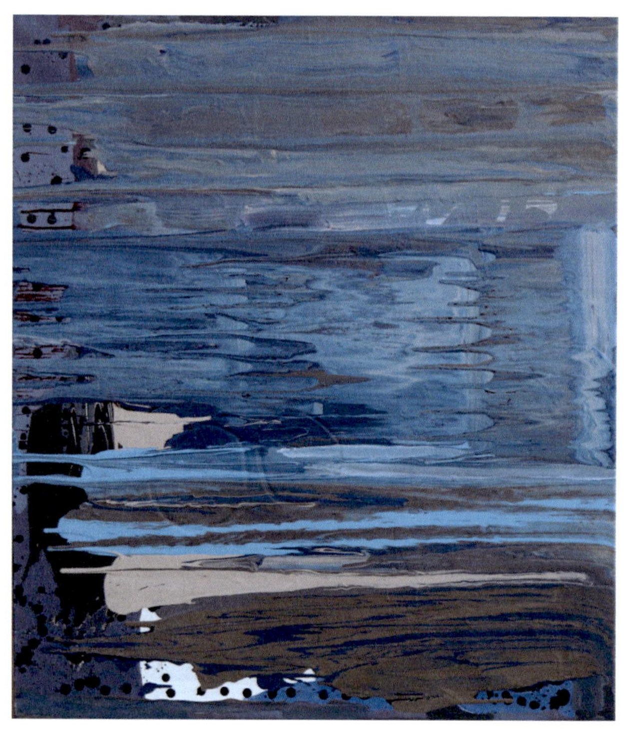

248
Acrylic on canvas (framed)
2009–2017
38 x 34 in (97 x 87 cm)

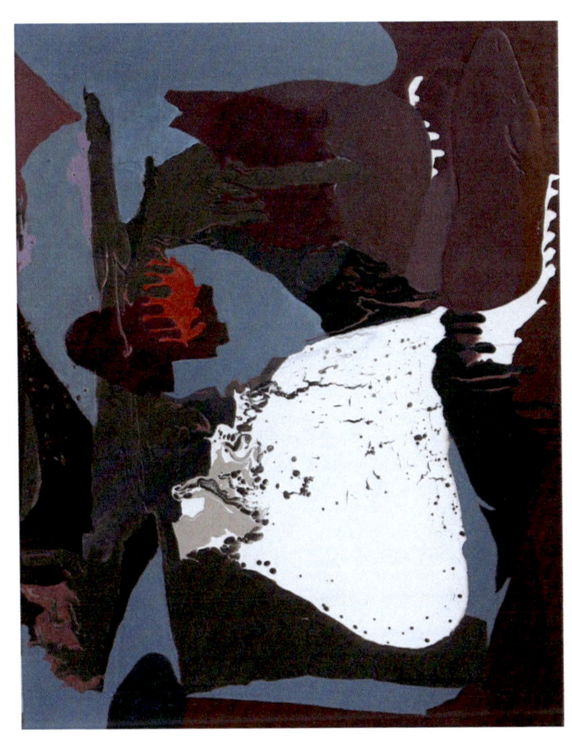

251
Acrylic on canvas
2009–2018
47 x 38 in (120 x 97 cm)

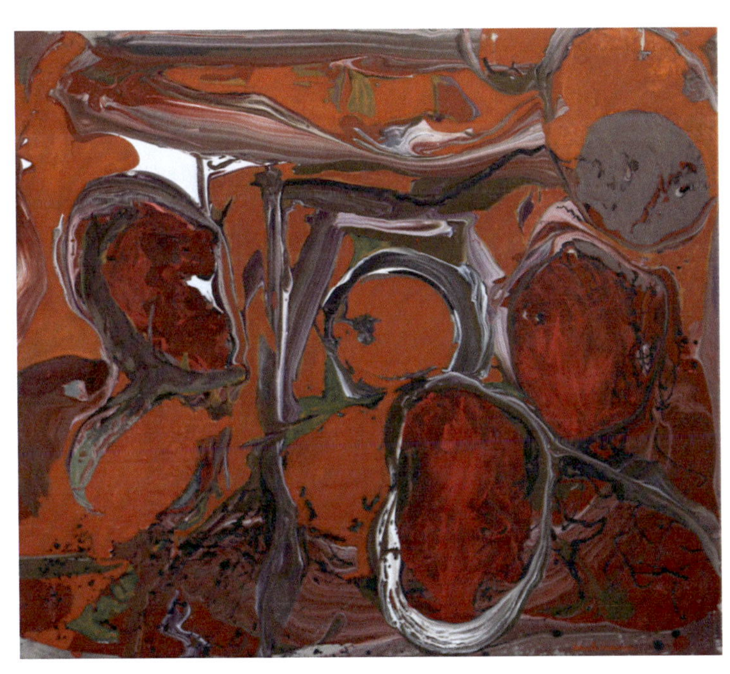

253
Acrylic on canvas
2009–2013
39.5 x 46 in (101 x 117 cm)

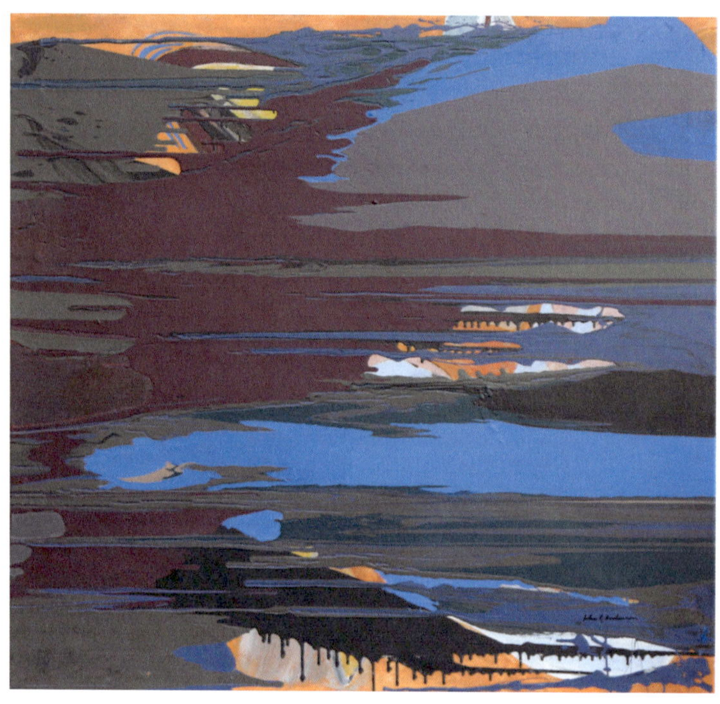

261
Acrylic on canvas
2009
44 x 48 in (112 x 122 cm)

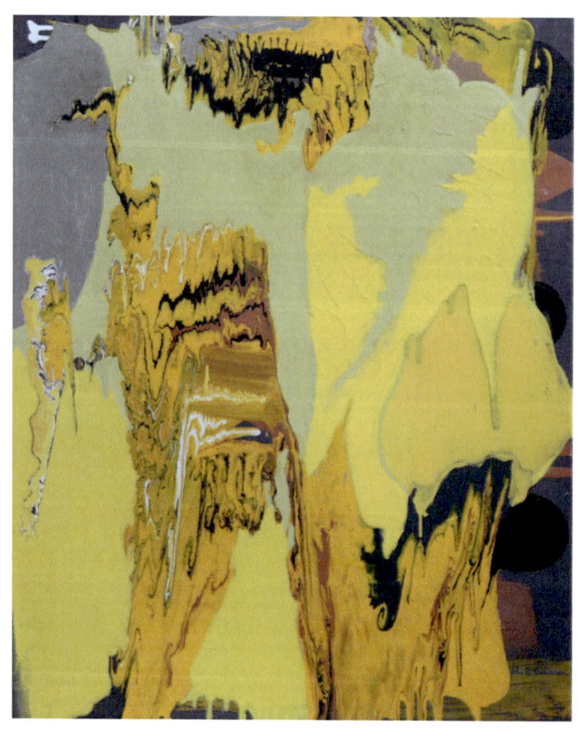

265
Acrylic on canvas
2009–2018
44.8 x 36.8 in (114 x 94 cm)

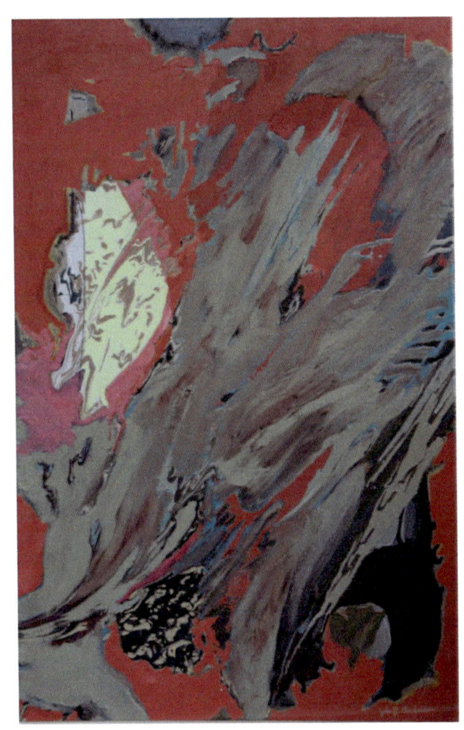

269
Acrylic on canvas
2009–2018
55.5 x 36 in (141 x 92 cm)

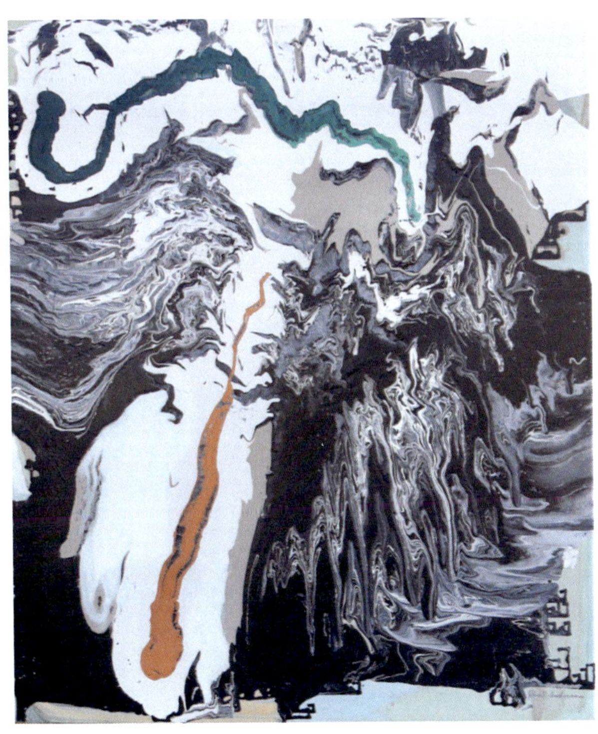

276
Acrylic on canvas (framed)
1997–2009
45 x 39 in (115 x 99 cm)

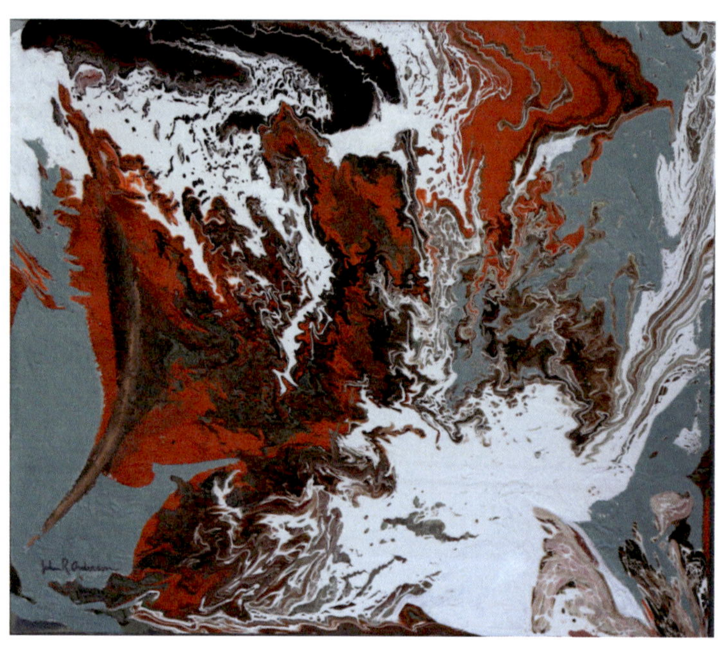

289
Acrylic on canvas (framed)
2007–2014
30 x 35 in (75 x 88 cm)

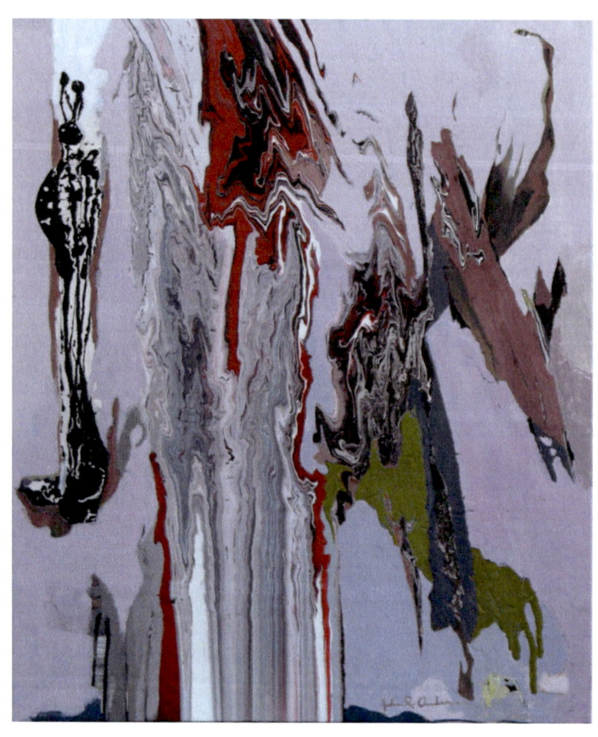

292
Acrylic on canvas
2009–2018
35 x 30 in (89 x 76 cm)

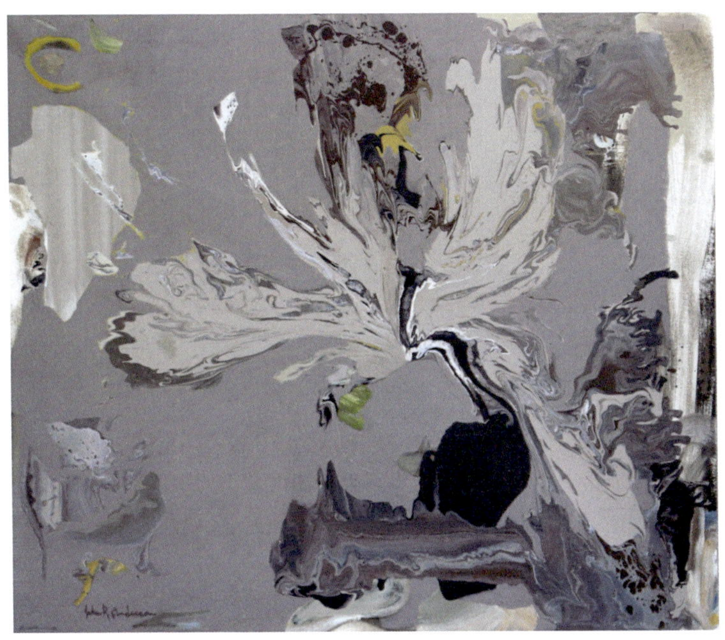

301
Acrylic on canvas (framed)
2010–2018
45.5 x 53 in (116 x 135 cm)

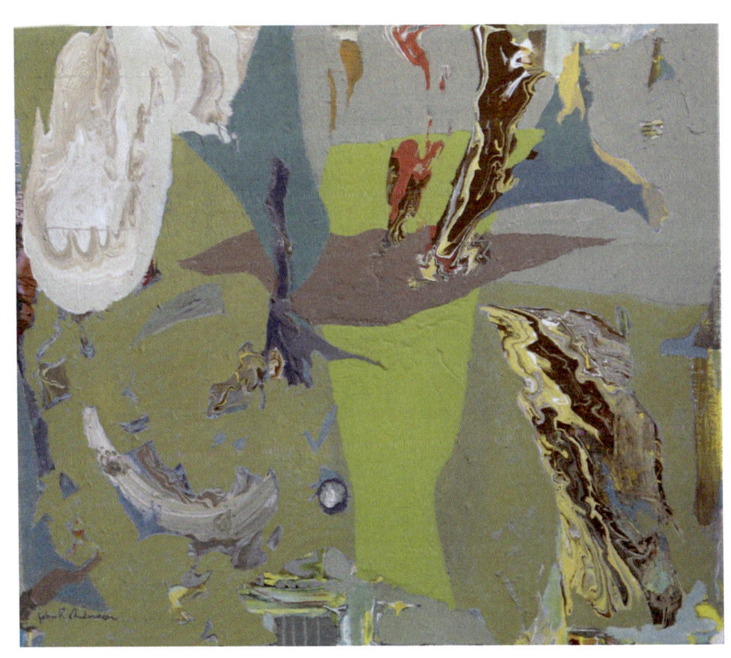

304
Acrylic on canvas (framed)
1998–2018
37.5 x 44 in (96 x 112 cm)

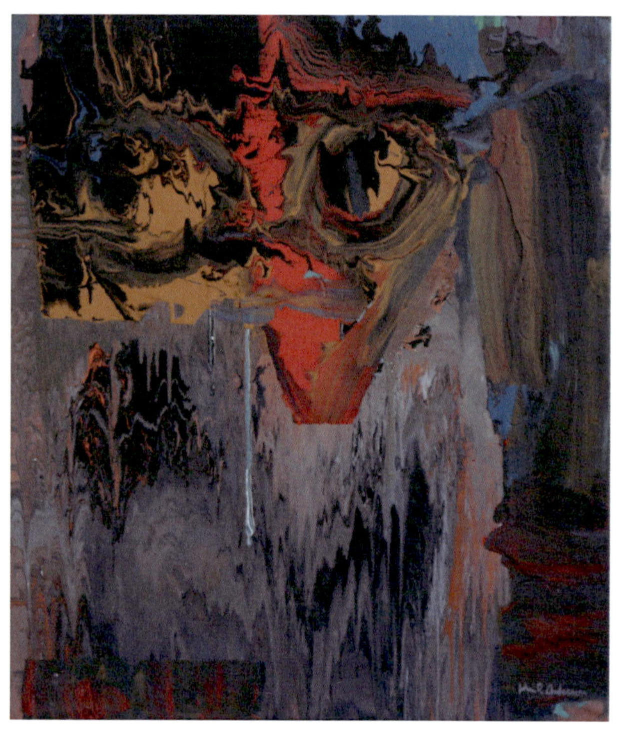

309
Acrylic on canvas
2012–2014
44 x 39 in (112 x 99 cm)

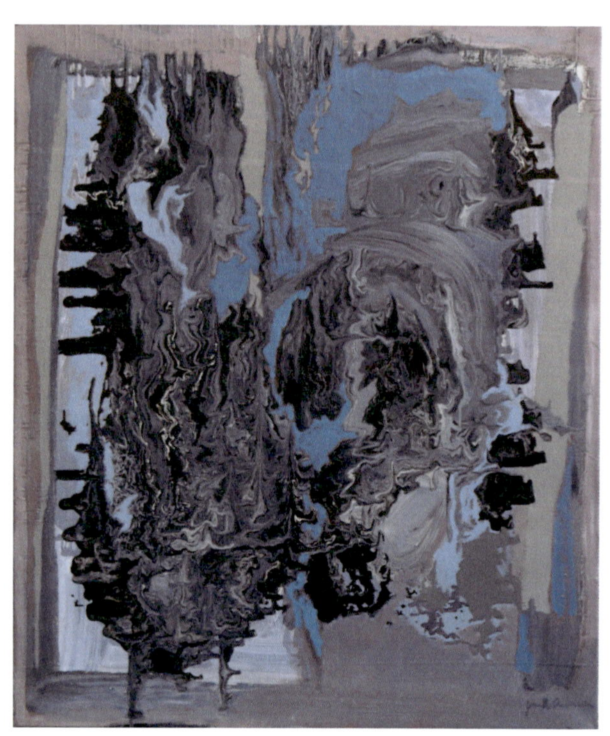

309.1
Acrylic on canvas
2011–2018
43.5 x 38 in (111 x 97 cm)

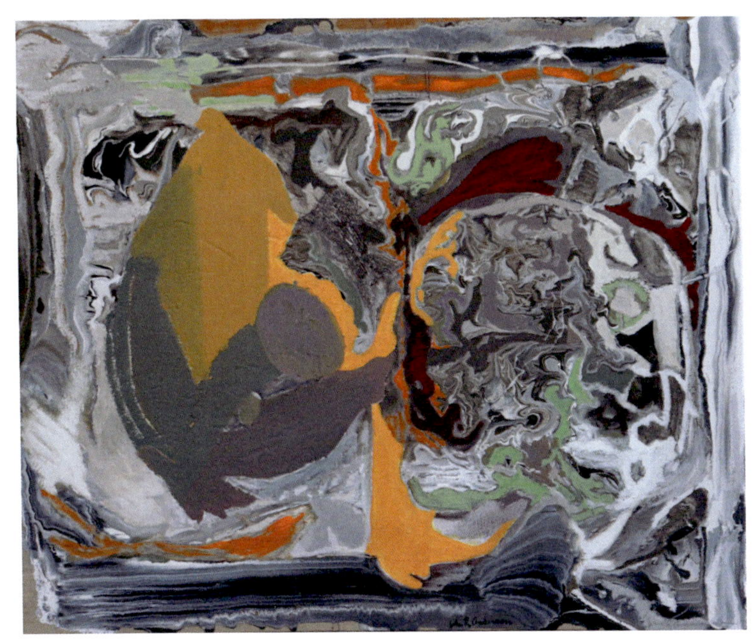

313
Acrylic on canvas
2011–2018
36 x 44 in (92 x 112 cm)

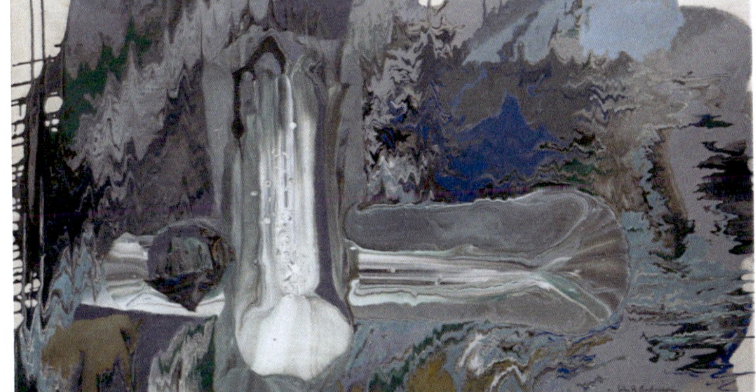

315
Acrylic on canvas
2013
28 x 52.5 in (71 x 134 cm)

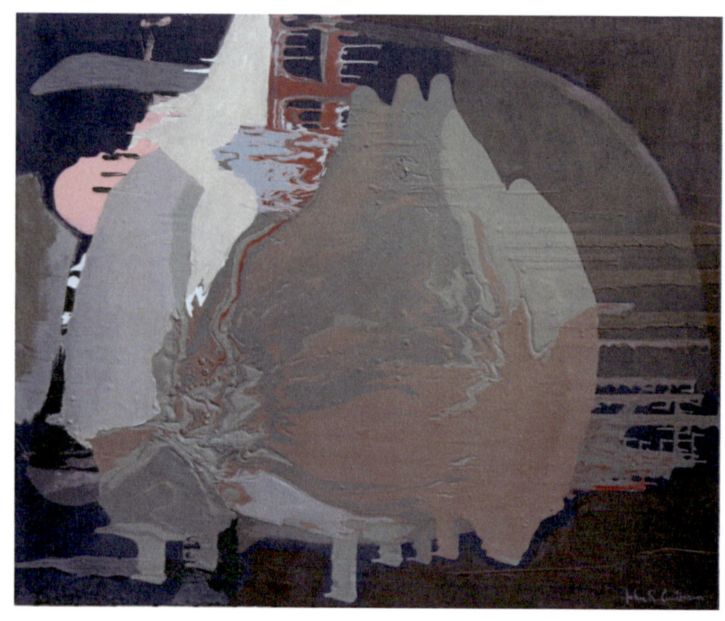

322
Acrylic on canvas
2013–2014
39 x 48 in (99 x 122 cm)

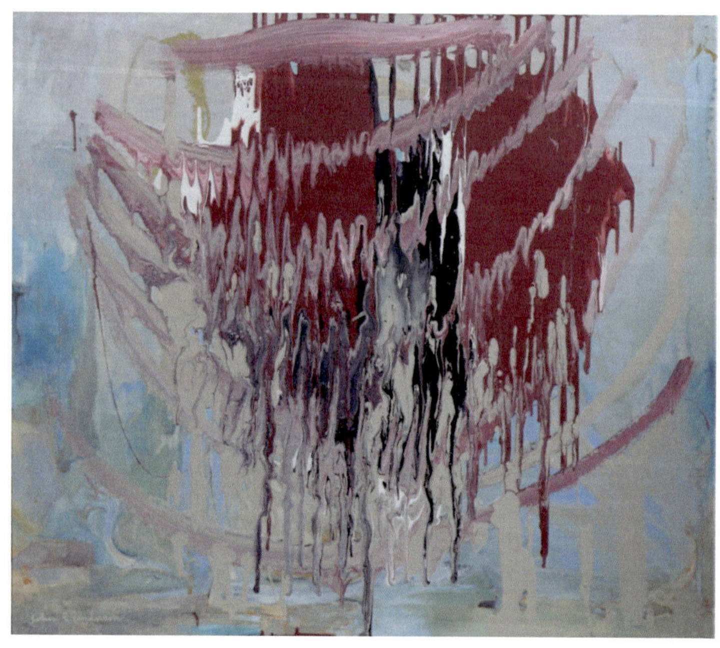

337
Acrylic on canvas
2013
48 x 56 in (122 x 142 cm)

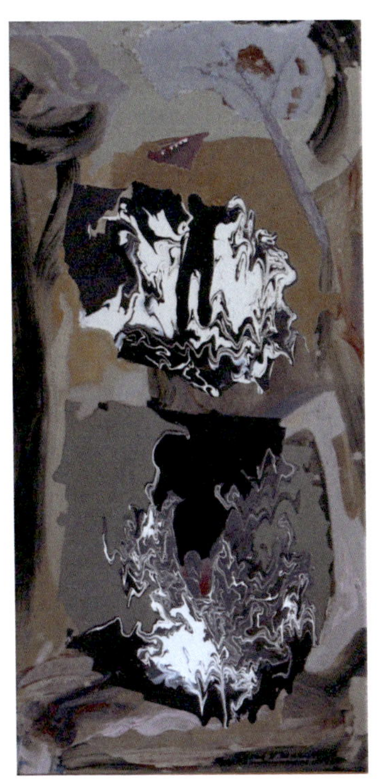

Rain Forest II
Acrylic on canvas (framed)
1992–2018
54 x 27 in (137 x 69 cm)

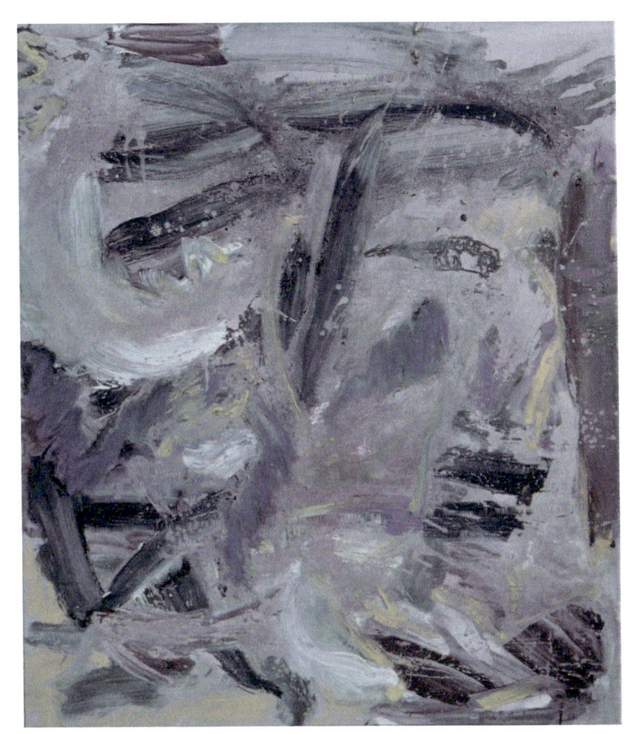

The Enemy is Us
Acrylic on canvas (framed)
1992
50 x 44 in (127 x 112 cm)

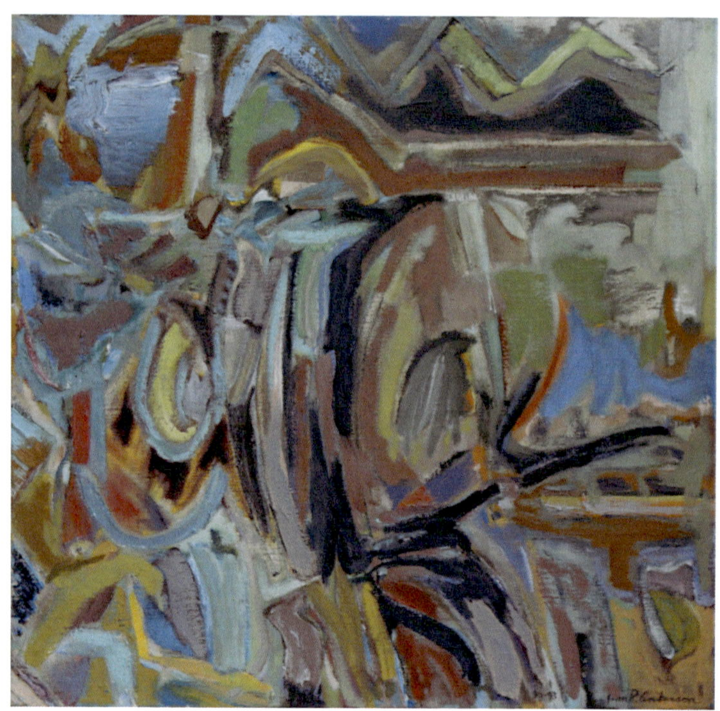

Untitled
Acrylic on canvas (framed)
1990–1993
21.5 x 22.5 in (55 x 57 cm)

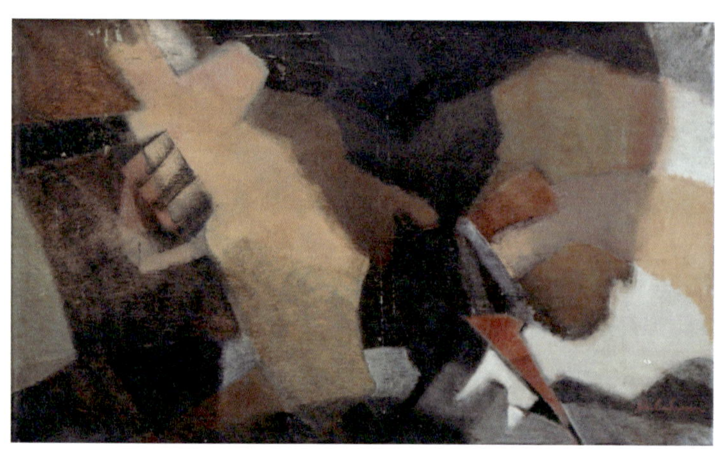

The Gift
Oil on canvas (framed)
1965
20 x 34 in (51 x 87 cm)